DEAR P.S. POOCH

DEAR P.S. POOCH

Advice For All Canine Cousins

Karl K. Stevens, Ph.D.

based on the advice columns of Princess and Simone Stevens

authorHOUSE®

AuthorHouse™
1663 Liberty Drive
Bloomington, IN 47403
www.authorhouse.com
Phone: 1-800-839-8640

© 2014 Karl K. Stevens, Ph.D. All rights reserved.

Cover Photo, Work Break, by Karl Stevens
Illustrations by Robin E. Coalson

No part of this book may be reproduced, stored in a retrieval system, or transmitted by any means without the written permission of the author.

Published by AuthorHouse 11/14/2014

ISBN: 978-1-4969-3923-4 (sc)
ISBN: 978-1-4969-3924-1 (e)

Library of Congress Control Number: 2014920245

Any people depicted in stock imagery provided by Thinkstock are models, and such images are being used for illustrative purposes only. Certain stock imagery © Thinkstock.

This book is printed on acid-free paper.

Because of the dynamic nature of the Internet, any web addresses or links contained in this book may have changed since publication and may no longer be valid. The views expressed in this work are solely those of the author and do not necessarily reflect the views of the publisher, and the publisher hereby disclaims any responsibility for them.

To Mom

Contents

Family and Friends 1

The Pet Person
Terrorists
Chasing Squirrels
Being Boarded
Airhead Party Pooches
Hissy Fit
Puppy Kindergarten
Yorkshire Terriers
Canines Vis-à-Vis Dogs
Magic for Mutts
Adoption?
Magic Can Happen
Our Own Home Someday?
Adoption I
Adoption II
Adoption III
Adoption IV
Without My Puppies

Cats 23

Canines and Catnip
Garfield
Cataholics Anonymous
Pavlov's Dog
Felines Vis-à-Vis Cats
The Litter Box
One Big Happy Family
Too Tough on Felines?
Egyptian Gods
Seeing-Eye Cat

Entertainment 33

Harley Hounds
Off Leash
Keep off the Beach
Ode to a Leash
Hemingway Hound
Possum Prowl
Chasing Cars
Possum Prowl Gone Wrong
Bowwow Blues
Canine Country Chorale
Head out the Window
Oh Give Me a Home
Reprimand

Food 49

    Ducks
    Cuisine Variety
    Pubs
    Poochie Popcorn
    Canine Caviar
    You Eat Bugs?
    Dinosaur Views
    Beef Bones
    Eating Out
    The Frankfurter
    Comeuppance
    Ingenuity in Action
    Eating Grass
    Shared Greens
    Omnivores, not Carnivores

Famous Canines in History 65

    The Great Houndini
    Favorite Dog Stories
    Your Bias Is Showing
    Canines for Khan
    Polly Podengo
    Curly Khan
    Toto
    Firehouse Dogs
    Enough Already!

Health and Aging 76

Cat Scan
Not Enough to Eat
Healer Hound
Doggie DNA
Where's My Treasure?
Service Dogs
All Work and No Play
Pet Purgatory
Therapy Dogs
Grounded
Moochie Poochie
Mellowing with Age

I. Family and Friends

Karl K. Stevens, Ph.D.

Dear P. S. Pooch:

Try as I might, my new master and I are just not getting along. He says I am the worst pet he has ever had and that he will never buy another purebred. Advice please!

Lisa Llapso

Lisa, Lisa, Lisa!

You need more than advice. We are e-mailing our response to you because you need help—and fast!

At the risk of insulting your parents or the breeder who raised you, where did you get the cockamamie idea that your human is the master and you are the pet? Everyone knows who the master of your household is—you are! Don't forget that. And don't let your human forget either.

This may not be easy. The urge to please—passed down to us from some nefarious ancestor—is strong. Self-control is essential. Humans also have an urge to please, and that is the secret to your eventual success. We suggest you start by always using the proper terminology, *pet person*, when referring to your human.

Write again and let us know how things are going. Good luck!

Karl K. Stevens, Ph.D.

Dear P. S. Pooch:

My friends say I shouldn't read your column because you are terrorists, and terrorists are bad. Is this true?

Dolly Daschund
Des Moines

Dolly, Dolly, Dolly!

We are *terriers,* not terrorists! Aside from kicking a little kitty butt now and again, we are total pacifists.

Dear P. S. Pooch:

I love to chase squirrels but am concerned that I am not living up to my heritage as a purebred rat terrier. What do you think?

Ronald

Ronnie,

We think you need glasses! Have you taken a good look at squirrels lately? They are nothing but overtailed rats with an orthodontics problem. Close enough for heritage's sake. Go for it.

P.S. You may enjoy our new self-improvement offering, *Chase without Guilt*, now available on videotape or CD. Order from our website or send $19.95, plus $4.95 for shipping and handling.

Karl K. Stevens, Ph.D.

Dear P. S. Pooch:

My pet persons are going on a trip, and they say I'll be boarded. Am I going to be spanked? I haven't done anything bad!

Leery in Louisiana

Dear Leery:

First, congratulations on your use of the proper terminology, *pet person(s)*. We bet you are an avid reader, right?

No, you are not going to be spanked. Boarding means you will stay at a special place like a hotel for canines. We think you will like it. You will have lots of attention and many cousins to play with. Some places even have a swimming pool and give massages! If you think you may need them, take a security blanket and a few of your favorite toys. Then relax and enjoy!

Dear P. S. Pooch:

My friends and I think your column is a joke and that you two are just airhead party pooches. Or maybe you're a couple of strays trying to pick up some easy coin with your dumb column. Have you ever done anything worthwhile?

Alfred von Humboldt XIX

Dear Mr. Humboldt:

What's this all about, Alfie? Cat eat out of your dish again? Embarrass yourself on the carpet?

We recognize your letter for what it is—a plea for help, probably brought on by the realization that we canines go from puppyhood to old age in a few brief years. Life is short, so relax and enjoy. We suggest you try transcendental meditation. Try using *parteeee* for your mantra, or choose another one you like from our self-improvement publication, *One Hundred Great Meditative Mantras for Mutts*. A complimentary copy is in the mail.

And Alfie, if you don't like our column, why do you read it?

Karl K. Stevens, Ph.D.

Dear P. S. Pooch:

My pet person says he is getting a big snake. What would you do if a snake came to live with you?

Skeptical in Seattle

Dear Skeptical:

If a snake came to live with us? We would have a hissy fit!

Dear P.S. Pooch:

You two seem to enjoy life so much. Have you ever had any bad experiences?

Wondering in Walla Walla

Dear Wondering:

We are normal canines who have had our share of bad experiences. One of the worst was puppy kindergarten. That's where we first encountered that ugliest of four-letter words—*obey*.

Karl K. Stevens, Ph.D.

Dear P. S. Pooch:

My friends and I, all Yorkies, read your column regularly. Can you tell us how our breed came to be known as Yorkshire terriers?

Admirers in Amarillo

Dear Admirers:

It all goes back to our alma mater, Yorkshire University. In the late 1800s, our rugby team—known for their ferocious level of play—were called the Yorkshire Terrors. The university administration, ever mindful of public and alumni relations, used the guise of a typographical error to change the name to Yorkshire Terriers. The name stuck, endowments soared, and the rest is history.

P.S. Glad you enjoy our column.

Dear P. S. Pooch:

Why do you go to such lengths to refer to us as canines? Why don't you just call us dogs?

Confused

Dear Confused:

It's a matter of respect. Humans often use the word *dog* in a negative sense—bad dog, dirty dog, and the like. Have you ever heard one say, "Bad canine" or "Dirty canine"?

Karl K. Stevens, Ph.D.

Dear P. S. Pooch:

I'm a widow with six beautiful puppies. It's a struggle to keep them fed, and I have nothing left for a holiday gift. It helps just to be able to tell someone. Thank you for listening.

Sad Sadie

Dear Sadie:

Congratulations on your beautiful family and your concern for the little ones. Puppies like magic, so we are sending you one of our *Magic for Mutts* kits. It comes complete with an illustrated instruction book and materials for 250 tricks and illusions. We hope the little whippers enjoy it. Bless you and your family.

Dear P. S. Pooch:

I overheard my pet persons talking, and I think I'm going to be put up for adoption. My home isn't perfect, but I certainly wouldn't want to lose it. I'm scared and don't know what to do. Should I run away? Or sign up with an online matching agency?

Trembling in Toronto

Dear Trembling:

We understand your concern. The ideas you mentioned would be acts of desperation, and you certainly don't want to make anything like that your opening move. Stay calm and alert, and focus on being a good dog. But don't overdo it; sucking up is counterproductive.

These things often have a way of working out for the better, so keep the faith. And maybe you misunderstood and there is no actual cause for concern.

Good luck!

Karl K. Stevens, Ph.D.

Dear P. S. Pooch:

Your advice to Trembling in Toronto was spot on!

I had seven homes before I was two years old, and along the way, I lost my right eye. But I always knew I had a lot to offer, so I just focused on being a good dog and tried my best to fit in. Then I caught my big break.

I now live in a nice house in the country with lots of neat places to rest, relax, and watch my animal and birdie friends. There are woods nearby where I can run, jump, and explore. The food is great. I provide entertainment and guard the house—and give plenty of pooch smooches. My pet person wrestles and plays with me and treats me with love and respect. We work well as a team; he gives me a treat, and I eat it.

Magic can happen!

Anonymous

Dear Anonymous:

Thank you for writing and sharing your experiences. A good home with love and respect is the most important thing in the world for all critters, humans included!

Dear P. S. Pooch:

We are a pack of thirteen strays, and we read your column every chance we get. We love learning about the lives and experiences of canine cousins. This helps us keep alive our dream that someday we, too, can have a home.

The Pack

Dear Pack:

For once, we don't know what to say or how to respond. May you all stay healthy and happy and have a good life!

Dear Readers:

You have slammed us with letters and questions about adoption and finding a good home. Our longtime friend Ralph went through this awhile back and documented his thoughts and feelings in four letters over time to his original pet persons. We think his words may be of some help or comfort for many of you, and he has kindly agreed to allow us to share them with you. We'll publish one letter each week. Here's the first.

Karl K. Stevens, Ph.D.

Ralph's First Letter:

Well, folks, it's getting along toward evening now, and my first day at my new home is just about over. It sure has been a long day.

My new people seem nice, but I'm not sure how this is going to work out. A good tummy rub is what I need most right now, and they don't seem to have a clue.

You know, before you came to pick me up at the puppy farm that morning, my mother told me that bad things happen sometimes when you go to live with humans. She said that if that happened to me, I should just make the best of it and try to understand. But I don't understand! I tried so hard to be a good dog. I loved you and thought you liked me too. I'll never know why you sent me to a new home.

I really hate to ask this, but I'm feeling kind of desperate right now and figure I don't have much to lose. Is there any chance I could come home soon?

Your dog always,

Ralph

P.S. If you get another dog, could you please not let him or her sleep in that old round bed of mine? I'd like to keep it as my very own special little place in the world.

Dear readers, here is Ralph's second letter:

Well, folks, it's been over two weeks since I wrote, and I haven't heard from you. I suppose you are very busy, as usual, and haven't had time to write. I was so hoping for a nice letter, or even better, a note just saying, "Come home."

I'm still not sure how things are going to work out here. The food is good and I get to sleep on the bed, which is nice. But my new people treat me like a baby and call me little Ralphie. I never wanted you to know, but I actually liked it when you called me fuzz butt and God's gift to fleas. I miss that, and I miss you.

Not much has been happening around here, so I don't have much else to say besides please write.

Your dog,

Ralph

P.S. I hope that old round bed of mine is tucked safely away in the closet. Who knows, maybe I'll need it again soon? Ha! Ha!

Dear readers, here is Ralph's third letter:

Well, folks, it's been almost three months since I last wrote, and I still haven't heard from you. How are you? I am fine.

Things are working out pretty well for me. It is fall here now. The leaves are so pretty, and the squirrels are fat and a bit slower than they were. I've made friends with the cat that lives next door, and we have fun chasing them up the trees. We make faces at them when they chatter at us.

My new people have turned out to be really nice, and they take very good care of me. Best of all, they do not go off and leave me alone all the time. Some new kids moved in next door, and they give great tummy rubs. The hair on my poor old tummy is just about worn off. How much can one hound take?

Write when you have time. I would love to hear from you.

Yours,

Ralph

P.S. Please say hello to that old round bed of mine and give it a love pat for me.

Dear readers, here is Ralph's fourth and final letter. Please let us know if things like these letters are of interest or help.

Well, folks, it's been almost a year since we last saw each other. I just want to tell you that little Ralphie said with love and affection is better than fuzz butt without. I now understand why you sent me to a new home. Thank you!

Best wishes,

Ralph

P.S. You might want to burn that old round bed of mine. You probably didn't notice, but it was loaded with fleas.

Dear Readers:

We realize our columns of late have been lengthy, but we hope you have found them to be interesting and helpful. We want to share one more piece with you—sent to us by our pet person on the fifth anniversary of our column—and then we'll reel in the rhetoric. Thanks for your patience.

Karl K. Stevens, Ph.D.

Without My Puppies

Without my puppies, I wouldn't be known as "chicken man" by the clerk at the nearby supermarket deli.

Without my puppies, I may never have known how fast cats can run or how quickly and high they can climb.

Without my puppies, I would have missed the possum parade along the backyard wall at 2:00 a.m. on that clear, crisp spring night.

Without my puppies, I wouldn't have met Fred, the portly shopping mall security guard—the former law student, policeman, professional wrestler, and now keen observer of life—the one who keeps dog treats in the dash pocket of his golf cart.

Without my puppies, I wouldn't have seen the back kitchen door of that restaurant where otherwise I may have dined.

Without my puppies, I couldn't have imagined the ecstasy of a tummy rub or good scratch.

Without my puppies, I wouldn't have been bold enough to say hello to that beautiful lady, the one with cleavage beyond my wildest imagination.

Without my puppies, I wouldn't have realized that stinky stuff has its place in this world—that yucky bits can be delectable if aged and prepared properly.

Without my puppies, I wouldn't have known the therapeutic value of giving others a good woofing now and then.

Without my puppies, how would I have realized the primordial joy of an occasional howl at the moon?

Without my puppies, I wouldn't have met Sergio, the kindly headwaiter at a local restaurant—the one who turns a blind eye to frequent nibbles from the chef's herb garden.

Without my puppies, I wouldn't have met the young homeless man—the one who can quote Chaucer but doesn't know the day of the week and who suffered mightily when he was struck on his bike by a hit-and-run driver.

Without my puppies, I wouldn't have considered bugs and lizards, or birds and squirrels, as friends and playmates.

Karl K. Stevens, Ph.D.

Without my puppies, I wouldn't have learned that a true measure of freedom is being able to piddle in your own backyard.

Without my puppies, I may have forgotten what it's like to be young, small, and dependent.

Without my puppies, when would I have come to the realization that a warm bed, good food, and love are all you really need for a fulfilling life?

Without my puppies, I may not have learned to pray for the healing hand of the universe.

Congratulations, girls, on five great years of Dear P. S. Pooch!

II. Cats

Karl K. Stevens, Ph.D.

Dear P. S. Pooch:

My good friend Buford says he likes catnip. I keep telling him that canines don't like catnip, but he won't stop. This is very irritating. How can I make him listen to me?

Miffed Muffy in Missoula

Dear Muffy:

Sorry, but we don't agree with you. All canines we know, including yours truly, love a little catnip now and then—a little nip on the tail, a little nip at the heels.

We think Buford is pulling your leg. You don't want to lose a good friend, so lighten up and enjoy the joke.

Dear P. S. Pooch:

I've been reading Garfield in the comic strip. His manners are awful, and he is always playing mean tricks on Odie. I think he is horrible. What do you think of him?

Wondering

Dear Wondering:

Garfield? He's a cat. Enough said!

Karl K. Stevens, Ph.D.

Dear P. S. Pooch:

Despite attending Cataholics Anonymous for years, I still get the occasional urge to kick kitty butt. Is there any hope for me?

Rolf

Note to our readers: We hope you are not offended by Rolf's language. We print all letters exactly as received, without editing. Of course, this means that some of your letters can't be used in a family publication.

Dear Rolf:

Don't be too hard on yourself. Studies have shown that the urge to chase cats, within moderation, is a sign of sound mental health. We ourselves indulge occasionally.

The reason for this urge is simple. Because of our superior intellect, canines were the first animals to be domesticated. Humans then used us to chase away varmints, particularly lions, tigers, leopards, and other feline critters. If felines had been brighter, humans would have domesticated them first, and we now would have cats chasing dogs. Laughable, isn't it?

So Rolf, you can enjoy an occasional chase without guilt. Just don't push it too far. And lay off the family cat.

Dear P. S. Pooch:

The cat I live with is snooty and is constantly telling me how great felines are. Can you help me with a snappy comeback?

Needs Help in Nebraska

Dear Needy:

We wouldn't exactly call it living if you have to share your abode with a cat. But that's an item for another day.

Try mentioning a famous canine, and see if that doesn't help put litter-head in his place. For example, there is Boris, the Russian wolfhound who lived in St. Petersburg, Russia, at the turn of the twentieth century. Boris was able to train his pet person, Ivan Pavlov, to ring a bell and bring him food whenever he salivated. Thus was born the concept of the conditioned reflex.

Dear P. S. Pooch:

I'm a feline, and all my friends and I enjoy your column. You are very biased, but we attribute that to the inferior intellect of dogs—yes, I said dogs. So why don't you wise up and start referring to us as felines instead of cats?

Miss Kitty

Meow, Meow Miss Kitty:

As we said in an earlier column, it's a matter of respect.

Dear P. S. Pooch:

Okay, you two, your feeble response to my recent letter has cost you some loyal readers and has prompted me to take drastic action. I am starting my own column for my feline friends, and dogs will be a hot topic. Think I'll call it *The Litter Box*. We'll send you a complimentary copy, but I don't think you'll like it.

Miss Kitty

Dear P. S. Pooch:

I'm a canine, but I think you are way too tough on felines. There are two dogs and three cats in our household, and we all get along great. We eat together, play together, and sleep together. So why don't you back off on the kitty bashing?

Randy

Dear Randy:

To each his own. Congratulations on being in such a happy, sane family. We live in a neighborhood loaded with feral cats, and they aren't the friendliest bunch in town. Perhaps that has colored our opinion of a lower life form. By the way, that kittie kibble is tasty, isn't it, Randy?

Dear P. S. Pooch:

We felines are sick and tired of hearing you canines brag about all your ties to ancient Egypt. Don't you know that the Egyptians actually had a cat god named Bast, protector of children? The best you guys could do was Anubis, a human with the head of a jackal and protector of the dead. No contest here!

We Win!

Dear We Win-Not:

If canines were so insignificant, why are we pictured on so many hieroglyphics and other records? And surely you've heard of the Pharaoh Hound? Truth told, you felines were hanging around the palace looking prissy while we were out in the field chasing game, riding in chariots, and joining in battles.

Karl K. Stevens, Ph.D.

Dear P. S. Pooch:

I share my home with a feline. He keeps telling me that he works harder than I do, is smarter than I am, and has better eyesight and hearing. Is this true? I'm starting to feel inferior.

Questioning

Dear Questioning:

What a joker! This cat is just pulling your tail. For starters, research shows that cats sleep 80 percent of the day—not exactly workaholics. Cats do have a better sense of hearing (did we hear a mouse scrambling around?) and see well up close. We can detect motion a mile away and can smell in 3D, IMAX, and Technicolor. Our snozzes are 100 million times more sensitive than that of humans, and our job skills are almost as diverse.

Cats evolved as loners, a factor that doesn't foster intelligence. To put it another way, have you ever heard of a seeing-eye cat?

III. Entertainment

Dear P. S. Pooch:

My friends and I like to ride with our pet persons, and we have formed a new club called the Harley Hounds. We are sending you two honorary memberships. Hope to see you at one of our meetings. Love that leather and those studs!

Road Rats

Dear Road Rats:

Thank you for the memberships to your club. About seeing us at a meeting—don't hold your breath.

Dear P. S. Pooch:

My pet person and I have had many arguments over whether I can walk off leash. When I get frustrated, I write poetry. My latest is a little ditty called *I Think I'll Be Me*. I'm sending the last few verses. Let me know what you think. I can send the rest if you wish.

I Think I'll Be Me
If I were a puppy,
All bouncy and round,
Would I sleep in a bed?
Would I sleep on the ground?

Would I have a furry coat
And maybe a pretty hat?
Could I chase rainbows,
Perhaps a kitty cat?

Would I be sleepy,
And where would I pee?
This is too complicated;
I think I'll be me.

Dear PO'd:

First things first. We think your pet person is just concerned about your safety, and you should be mighty thankful for that. Perhaps your friends know of some dog parks or other places nearby where you safely can be off-leash.

As to the poetry, the sample you sent is sufficient.

Dear P. S. Pooch:

The city in which I live has a beautiful beach, but we canines aren't allowed to go there. We aren't even allowed on the sidewalk on the beach side of the street! Several weeks ago I crossed over to the beach side to get a closer look at the beautiful surf and was collared by a city policeman. He had the smell of cat all about him, and I wasn't surprised that he ignored my pleas for lenience. Now I have to appear before a Judge Catz for a hearing on violation of a city ordinance. I just don't think this is fair, do you?

Surfer Pup

Dear Surfer:

Fair or not, your immediate concern is the hearing. Believe us, you don't want to end up spending time in the puppy slammer. Call your local chapter of the CCLU (Canine Civil Liberties Union) and tell them you have immediate need of canine counsel to represent you.

Dear P. S. Pooch:

My sister and I were delighted to read the letter from PO'd about wanting to be off-leash. We share the same dream, and we too have expressed our frustration in verse. May we share it with your readers?

Over-Constrained

Ode to a Leash
Oh leash of mine,
You long black thing
That binds us to the here and now, the what is.
It's the what might be
We want to see,
So off, off, off from me!

Dear Over-Constrained:

Thanks for writing, but did you not read our response to PO'd?

Now readers, enough letters about leashes and such. The desire for freedom runs rampant in all creatures!

Dear P. S. Pooch:

I'm a writer and would like your opinion of my work. Here's a small sample.

Hemingway Hound

The night was dark and stormy. Sheets of wind-driven rain sliced through my furry coat as I moved steadily onward through the dark, testing every step, lest I miss the meandering of the hill crest and plunge into the dark waters below. Somewhere ahead, Ol' Blue, descended of a long line of champion Blueticks, long of leg and sleek of body, worked his craft. Then it happened, as it had happened to my ancestors long before me! The pungent smell of raccoon on wet leaves wafted on the breeze, tickling the primitive part of my brain, the message confirmed by Ol' Blue's mournful cry. I knew instantly he was on the trail—the trail of death.

Dear Hemingway:

Knock it off, Hemingway. We would recognize the prose of Billie Bluetick anywhere. And Billie, we have told you time and again, we don't like violence!

Karl K. Stevens, Ph.D.

Dear P.S. Pooch:

I'm planning a party for ten to twelve of my friends. Menus and decorations are set, but I'm having trouble deciding on entertainment. Any ideas for group activities we could do in my nice backyard?

Perle in Paducah

Dear Perle:

Any ideas? My dear, this is P. S. Pooch you're asking! Here is our number one party favorite.

We think your group would love a possum prowl! Just remind your guests that the event is all in fun. If you check around, you should be able to locate a professional possum to work your party. They charge by the hour. Do check references, and do not pay in advance. If your guest of honor spends the night snoozing in a tree in your yard, it will cost you big bucks. Go forth, and have a ball!

Dear P. S. Pooch:

I have an insatiable urge to chase cars. My mother says I should forget it because my dad and seventeen uncles and cousins had mishaps with automobiles. But I am fast for my age, and I know I could do it. Am I possessed?

Fast Freddie in Fresno

Dear Freddie:

You're possessed all right—of mighty poor judgment! Haven't you seen the way people drive these days? And what would you do with one of those mechanical beasts if you did manage to catch it?

We suggest you try our new video game, *Chase*. You can choose among twenty-five different vehicles in ten different colors, operating on your choice of twenty different roadways at ten different speeds. Our favorite is the red Lamborghini on an alpine highway.

Dear P. S. Pooch:

I'm simply furious! I followed the advice you gave Perle in Paducah and had a possum prowl at my annual Halloween party. I paid the entertainer I hired $150, and he did nothing but play possum for three solid hours. My party was ruined, and my friends think I'm stupid. I'll never follow your lousy advice again!

Taken in Toronto

Dear Taken:

We're truly sorry about your party. However, our advice is like a prescription for an antibiotic—you are supposed to take it all. Remember, we said, "Check references, and do not pay in advance." And now you know why.

Dear P. S. Pooch:

When my dad passed away, I found many interesting things among his belongings, including this song he had written. We had no idea he was a songwriter. With your permission, our family would like to share this piece with your readers.

Bowwow Blues
Woke up late this morning
With beef bone on my breath.
Wouldn't eat a chicken bone,
That could mean my death.
Oh, I've got the bowwow blues.
Oooo, ooooah, oooo,
I've got the bowwow blues.

Politics are simmering,
The economy's heading south.
But I don't really give a damn
With this sweet bone in my mouth.
Oh, I've got the bowwow blues.
Oooo, ooooah, oooo,
I've got the bowwow blues.

Heard some people talking,
They say life's a –itch.
That sounds mighty good to me,
And now I've got the itch.
Oh, I've got the bowwow blues.

Oooo, ooooah, oooo,
I've got the bowwow blues.

Sad Puppy

Dear Sad:

We are so sorry to hear about your father's move to dog heaven. Any possibility that you inherited his songwriting ability?

Dear P. S. Pooch:

My pet person is big on Beethoven. I like music, but if I hear one more concerto, I'll have a howling fit. I need to hear something a bit more basic, if ya know what I mean.

Billie Bluetick

Dear Billie:

Nice to hear from you again. Yes, we know what you mean. Our pet person happens to be a Mozart maniac.

We greatly enjoy the new CD by our Canine Country Chorale. It features such hits as "Possum on the Wind," "Hungry Hound Blues," and "Momma Was a Purebred and Papa Was a Junkyard Dog." The nostalgia track features Elvis Presley and his big hit, "Hound Dog." Try it; we think you'll like it.

Karl K. Stevens, Ph.D.

Dear P. S. Pooch:

My pet person says she will let me ride in the car with my head out the window if I can give her one good reason for doing it. Try as I might, I can't come up anything. Help!

Constrained in California

Dear Constrained:

You want to do it because it is *fun*! Reason enough. Watch out for the bugs.

Dear P. S. Pooch:

My sister and I also are songwriters. Here's a few lines from a new number we are working on.

Oh give me a home, where the bunny rabbits roam,
And the sagebrush isn't a mile high,
Where never is heard, the discouraging *come* word,
And I can play until evening is nigh.

What do you think?

Pearl and Myrle

Dear P and M:

We didn't realize our readers were so talented! Our Country Music Chorale is always looking for new material. Contact information is on their website. Some of your lyrics may border on plagiarism, but their attorneys can handle all that.

Dear P. S. Pooch:

We can't believe the really bad (actually stupid) advice you gave Constrained. Auto window glass is nothing short of a guillotine in the event of sudden stops. And bouncing down the pavement after falling from an open vehicle, like a pickup, isn't exactly good for your health. Either practice is a death wish!

Canine Vehicular Safety Agency

Dear CVSA:

Our bad! We stand corrected. You probably can tell we don't imbibe ourselves.

IV. Food

Karl K. Stevens, Ph.D.

Dear P. S. Pooch:

I enjoy going to a pond near my home and watching and chasing ducks. Do you like ducks?

Wally Weimaraner
Westchester

Dear Wally:

We love ducks—preferably with a nice l'orange sauce!

Dear P. S. Pooch:

I'm tired of having the same food at every meal. Would it be wise to ask for some culinary variety? Could you mention a few of your favorite foods I might like to try?

Tasteless in Toronto

Dear Tasteless:

It seldom hurts to ask. Here are some of our favorites: beluga caviar on crisp points of toast; quiche Lorraine; low-fat Braunschweiger with side of grated Vidalia onion; and breast of range chicken sautéed in a fine vintage of your choice (we prefer Chablis—no cooking wine puhleeze!)

Karl K. Stevens, Ph.D.

Dear P. S. Pooch:

My brother and I are twin English bulldogs who lived in the UK for several years. We really miss the pub scene there. The cool, dim atmosphere was very relaxing and the patrons generous with bits of their goodies. We soon will be opening a similar establishment for canines in our neighborhood but are having trouble coming up with a good name. The ones we know—The Red Lion, Billy Goat Inn, Fox and Hounds, Slug and Lettuce, Sir Loin—just don't resonate. Any suggestions?

Edward and Charles

Dear Ed and Charlie:

How about Squirrel and Bone? Like it, and it's yours. Send notice of your grand opening, and we'll share it with our readers.

Dear P. S. Pooch:

I love popcorn, but my pet person says it is bad for me and won't let me have any. Is this true?

Orville

Dear Orville:

Sad but true. Most popcorn is bad for canines. We suggest a natural health food equivalent—bugs. We prefer lawn moths, common in our area in the spring. They are crunchy and have a slightly salty taste. We call them poochie popcorn. And they come with an added bonus. Running and jumping to catch them provides a great aerobic workout. You easily can burn more calories than you consume, which helps the old waistline. You may have to experiment a bit to discover what tasty critters are available in your area. Enjoy!

Karl K. Stevens, Ph.D.

Dear P. S. Pooch:

My friend Slobbers just returned from a camping trip with his family in Colorado. All he can talk about is the fantastic canine caviar he had there. I feel like an idiot. I have no idea what he is talking about, and it isn't in my dictionary. Help!

Puzzled Petunia in Pennsylvania

Dear Petunia:

Don't worry, you are not an idiot. In plain language, your friend is talking about deer poo, which you also have in Pennsylvania. The aroma and taste is very appealing to canines, but it can contain dangerous microbes and germs. Our advice is to play it safe and lay off. You'll also get a lot more pet person kisses if you do.

Dear P. S. Pooch:

Yuck, you guys eat bugs? How disgusting! And I thought you were classy dames.

Turned Off in Topeka

Dear Turned Off:

Don't rush to judgment. In many parts of the world, insects are an increasingly important part of the human diet. Try some—you may like them.

Karl K. Stevens, Ph.D.

Dear P. S. Pooch:

We're talking about canines here, kids, not humans.

Turned Off in Topeka

Dear Turned Off:

We are not trying to change your opinion. And please don't try to inflict your dinosaur views on other readers.

Dear P. S. Pooch:

After months of begging, my pet person finally relented and got me some beef bones. Sad to say, I didn't enjoy them as much as I had hoped. Were my expectations too high?

Disappointed in Dallas

Dear Disappointed:

It's the prices of beef, and not your expectations, that are too high. We suspect your pet person succumbed to the temptation to buy you a cheaper grade. You should always insist on USDA choice or prime.

Also, beef bones are best if properly aged. We bury ours in the backyard until they reach their peak of perfection and flavor. Wait for signs of flies or for an aroma your pet person finds disgusting. You may have to experiment with the timing. In the hot, humid south Florida climate in which we live, this takes about nineteen minutes.

Karl K. Stevens, Ph.D.

Dear P. S. Pooch:

Like Tasteless in Toronto, who wrote you earlier, I get tired of the same food all the time, so my friends and I go out and see what we can pick up elsewhere. Any suggestions on the best places to look?

Dining Out Dan

Dear Dan:

Variety is the spice of life, they say. Construction sites are good places to look, but watch out for chicken bones. It must be the universe's way of spiting canines, but construction workers seem to flock to chicken. Once in a while you'll run across a crew that likes ribs. Guard this site carefully.

Another good place to look is *around* Dumpsters and behind restaurants and grocery stores. Many choice goodies can be found here. Note the emphasis on around. You don't want to fall into a Dumpster and get trapped. And watch out for the broken glass. It seems to grow and flourish near these depositories.

Happy hunting!

Dear P. S. Pooch:

I am hoping you will join my friends and me in a battle to stamp out the disgusting human practice of calling one of their favorite foods, the frankfurter, a hot dog. This is a disgrace to our genus. Will you sign our petition to the US Food and Drug Administration asking them to stop this ugly practice?

Lizzie

Dear Lizzie:

Sorry to tell you, last we read the origin of the name *hot dog* remains a mystery. We admire your spunk, but with this uncertainty, we don't hold out a lot of hope for success of your petition.

Karl K. Stevens, Ph.D.

Dear P. S. Pooch:

I am a regular reader and usually enjoy your columns. However, at times you two can be the most unthinking, inconsiderate canines I have ever encountered. I refer to your snide remarks about the grade of beef bones in your letter to Disappointed in Dallas.

Has it ever occurred to you that the cheaper grades may be all that many of us can afford? My husband and I work four jobs to feed our puppies, and choice and prime beef are an extravagant luxury well beyond our reach.

Disappointed in Denver

Dear Disappointed:

You certainly gave us a well-deserved comeuppance! We always try to inject some humor into our responses to our readers. They say that humor bites. In this case, it bit us—in the hindquarters. Our apologies to all our readers.

Dear P. S. Pooch

May I share with your readers the unique way our group handles the combined problems of eating out and Dumpster security? Dumpsters are deathtraps. Don't go near them.

We teamed up with a group of raccoons in a local park, where picnickers leave many choice bits in the garbage cans. The raccoons are very nimble and scurry into the cans and throw out the goodies. We help gather them up and provide security. We all share the spoils. Laughably, many of the garbage cans bear a "Raccoon Proof" label.

Using the Old Noodle

Dear Noodle:

We love to hear about ingenuity in action!

Karl K. Stevens, Ph.D.

Dear P. S. Pooch:

I like to eat grass. There are a number of tasty varieties growing in our yard and neighborhood. My friends think I'm off my rocker. What do you think?

Greenie in Greenville

Dear Greenie:

Grass provides important nutritional elements, but do be very careful about where you harvest your treats. Humans have a tendency to use copious amounts of insecticide, which can be very harmful to your health—possibly even fatal. Our pet person gives us vegetables, which we absolutely love and which removes the dangers of picking up some contaminated grass. Maybe a solution for you?

Dear P. S. Pooch:

I have another possible solution for Greenie, if he has a cat in the family. Many humans provide cats with a supply of fresh-growing greens. I live with a cat, and he is great about letting me share his goodies. So far, our pet persons haven't caught on. Who says all cats are bad?

Shared Greens

Dear Shared:

Now we've heard just about everything! Whatever works for you.

Karl K. Stevens, Ph.D.

Dear P. S. Pooch:

Canines eating vegetables! Whatever is this world coming to? Don't you know we canines are carnivores, pure and simple?

President, Carnivores Anonymous

Dear Pres:

Not pure and simple. Actually, we are omnivores.

If you can climb down off your soapbox for a moment, take a gander at the list of ingredients on the bag, box, or can of food your pet person provides for you. Take an aspirin along with you—what you see may give you a headache.

V. Famous Canines in History

Karl K. Stevens, Ph.D.

Dear P. S. Pooch:

We are Jack Russells and loved your column about the Russian wolfhound who conditioned Pavlov to ring a bell and bring him food. Science is fascinating! Are there any famous ancestors up our family tree?

Jack and Jill

Dear Jack and Jill:

You are in luck! The Great Houndini, a Jack Russell terrier from Appleton, Wisconsin, was famous for his ability to escape from leashes, harnesses, cages, pens, and other forms of constraint. Hairy, as his friends knew him, traveled the country performing his feats as an escape artist.

Dear P. S. Pooch:

Do you like dog stories and books? What are some of your favorites? We like Lassie.

Parlor Full of Puppies

Dear Parlor Pooches:

We find Lassie to be a tad insipid. Our tastes run more toward the works of Jack London—*Call of the Wild, Jerry of the Islands, White Fang, Brown Wolf* ...

Our favorite is the story of Greyfriars Bobby. Bobby was a Skye terrier living in Edinburgh, Scotland, in the late 1800s. His pet person died and was buried in the local churchyard. Bobby went every night and slept on the grave until his death. Locals gave him food and water.

Our pet person told us that his mother gave him a book about Bobby when he was a little boy and that he was able to visit this churchyard three times over the years.

Some now say the story of Bobby is a hoax, perpetrated by a money-grabbing merchant. There are many well-documented instances of canine dedication beyond death of their pet persons, so we choose to believe the story of Bobby is true. Humans can be so inconsiderate of the dedication of us canines!

Dear P. S. Pooch:

Your bias is showing. Your columns on famous canines seem to favor our smaller cousins.

A Larger Specimen of the Canine Species

Dear Larger:

We wouldn't exactly call a Russian wolfhound small! However, being small ourselves, some bias on our part is possible. How about the story of Rin-Tin-Tin, a German shepherd rescued by an American soldier during WWI? Is Rinny large enough to suit you?

Soldiers shared their food with Rin-Tin-Tin. The food was stored in metal containers, which came to be known as tin cans. After the war, Rinny and his progeny went on to becomes stars of film, radio, and TV. Many lines of canine food and treats carry their endorsement.

Karl K. Stevens, Ph.D.

Dear P. S. Pooch:

I'm a history major at a local canine college, with a special interest in the middle ages. I would love to be able to tell my friends about some famous cousin from this era. Can you help?

Curious Canine

Dear Curious:

How about this? It is a little-known fact that canines were with Genghis Khan. They were part of a group called Canines for Khan. Larger cousins, likely mastiffs, actually joined his troops in battle.

Why Canines for Khan? Picture this—Mongol hordes sweeping across the steppes of Asia, with a herd of cats running alongside!

Dear P. S. Pooch:

I love your columns about famous canines in history, but so far, they are all about the guys. How about something for the gals?

Girlie Girl

Dear Girlie:

We respond to our readers' inquiries as we receive them. No preferential treatment intended. How about this story?

Polly was a Portuguese podengo pequeno who sailed aboard Christopher Columbus's flagship during his maiden voyage to the new world. Polly killed the rats that ate the grain that lay in the hold of the ship that Columbus built.

Karl K. Stevens, Ph.D.

Dear P. S. Pooch:

I'm so impressed you could give me information about canine cousins and Genghis Khan! I don't suppose you have any other tidbits to share and that I could use to impress my prof.

Curious Canine Back Again

Dear Back Again:

Sweetie, you're talking to P. S. Pooch here! We do have another morsel you may enjoy.

One of the Canines for Khan was the runt of his litter and ran with a hitch in his stride, so he could not join the others in battle. Genghis was mightily impressed with his efforts to overcome his disabilities, adopted him, and named him Curly Khan.

Curly hit upon the idea of cheering for Genghis and his troops and recruited others to help. Thus was born the concept of cheerleading. Versions of their most popular cheer, which translates as, "Genghis, Genghis, he's our man, if he can't do it no one can," are still heard today in schools and gyms across the land.

Dear P. S. Pooch:

Another famous canine in history for the gals, please. Maybe a movie star?

Advocate for the Ladies

Dear Addie:

We hear you. Have you heard about Terry, the female brindle terrier who played the role of Toto in the smash hit movie *The Wizard of Oz*? She was paid more that the human actors and now has a popular line of bathroom fixtures named after her character.

Karl K Stevens, Ph.D.

Dear P. S. Pooch:

I'm the headmistress of a puppy kindergarten. Our class watched the film *101 Dalmatians*, and now the students are asking how Dalmatians became firehouse dogs. I haven't a clue. Can you help?

Miss Muffett

Dear Muffie:

P. S. Pooch to the rescue! Early firehouses had horse-drawn pumpers, and there was need for individuals to run alongside the horses to clear the way through the crowds and to help keep them from being distracted by excited humans. Dalmatians bid on the job and won the contract.

Eventually motorized vehicles replaced horse-drawn pumpers. Because of the powerful union they had developed over the years, some Dalmatians remained on the job as mascots and continue in this role today.

Dear P. S. Pooch:

My friends and I can't get enough of your famous canines in history columns. More! More!

Insatiable in Iowa

Dear Insatiable:

You may not have had enough of famous canines in history, but we certainly have! There are so many famous canines that we could spend the rest of our lives writing about them.

To all our readers, enough already! Forget cats and food for a few moments, and get on your computer and Google!

VI. Health and Aging

Dear P. S. Pooch:

All my life, I've enjoyed a little canine-feline interaction, if you know what I mean. Now I'm older and my eyesight is dimming. I just can't spot the critters in the bushes like I used to. So to all you young puppies out there, enjoy your canine pleasures while you can—old age comes all too soon.

A Been-There Beagle

Dear Been-There:

We're sure our young readers will enjoy hearing from an old pro like you. But don't give up on yourself too soon.

We recently read about a new miniature radar device, called *Cat Scan*, that fits on your collar. It detects the presence of any cat within a 150-foot radius. That would give you plenty of time to plot your strategy and make your moves. Sounds like this would make a wonderful gift. Show this column to your pet person, and write and let us know how it works!

Dear P. S. Pooch:

I'm a young puppy with six brothers and sisters, and Mom is a little short on food. I'm hungry and don't think I'm getting enough to eat. What shall I do?

Puppy Number Seven

Dear Little Seven:

This is serious! You need good nutrition to grow up and become a strong, healthy canine. One of us (Simone) had this same problem. Fortunately, her puppy pet person saw the situation and fed her by hand. (That may be why she is overly fixated with humans—Princess speaking here.)

Do you think your mom and pet person are aware of your problem? If not, you need to make a ruckus and do anything you can to get their attention. Our prayers are with you. Good luck!

Dear P. S. Pooch:

My sister is always licking people. She particularly goes for cuts and sores, which I think is totally gross. I'm sick and tired of her constant sucking up! How can I make her stop?

Burned in Boca

Dear Burned:

Is that the ol' green-eyed monster we see lurking over your shoulder? Seriously, your sister's behavior is not an aberration of the urge to please, as you suggest. Your sister is a healer hound. The fact that she licks cuts and sores is the sure sign.

Healer hounds have an enzyme in their saliva that has great curative powers. They apply their craft by a laying on of tongues. Instead of being miffed, you should be honored to have a sister who is so gifted.

Karl K. Stevens, Ph.D.

Dear P. S. Pooch:

Most of my friends are purebreds, justifiably proud of their heritage. I'm a mixed breed and wasn't present at all the escapades that led to the current incredible me. I don't know what to say when friends ask about my background. Do you think the new DNA test I read about would help with this predicament?

Who In Whoville

Dear Who:

Don't be too tough on yourself. Notice that in all of literature, the word *purebred* is not spelled with a capital P.

The canine DNA test is relatively new technology, and users' opinions are varied. Some think it has given them great insight into their heritage while others think the letters DNA should stand for "does not apply." The tests are relatively inexpensive. If coin is not an issue, give it a try.

Dear P. S. Pooch:

I was excited to read your response to Been-There Beagle and to hear how technology is coming to the aid of us older folk. I'm referring to the *Cat Scan* you mentioned.

Memory is my problem. I can bury some treasure or choice bits and then spend hours trying to remember where I put them. This really frosts me. Any suggestions?

Where's It at Willie

Dear Willie:

Have we got good news for you and for others with your challenge! On the market now is a miniature voice-activated GPS device that clips to your collar. It works with our new cell phone app, available for download free from our website. One yip and a retrievable map locating your treasure appears on your cell phone. How's that for magic?

Dear P. S. Pooch:

I'm a guide dog, trained to alert my human companion to the onset of anxiety attacks. My friends are seeing-eye dogs. Does this mean we also are healer hounds?

Dedicated in Duluth

Dear Dedicated:

While you and your friends obviously have very special talents, you most likely are not healer hounds. If you read our earlier column, you know that healers use the curative powers of their saliva to overcome injury and disease. It is extremely rare for an individual to have both guide and healing talents at a professional level.

We compliment you and your friends for taking up such worthwhile careers. Too many of our canine cousins choose the life of street gangs, ignoring and wasting any talents with which they may have been blessed. You and your friends are excellent role models for puppies everywhere.

Dear P. S. Pooch:

Do you two ever do anything besides work?

Lazy in Longville

Dear Lazy:

Surely you've heard the old canine proverb, "All work and no play makes for a hapless hound." We engage in many physical activities and have a wide range of interests, including theatre and the arts.

We recently hosted the Great Lizzaro and his business partner, Chia Charlie, in town from the Bahamas for the local opening of their smash hit musical revue, *Thousand and One Leapin' Lizards*. It's a great show. Don't miss it if it comes to your town.

Karl K. Stevens, Ph.D.

Dear P. S. Pooch:

My sister and I enjoyed the holidays a bit too much, and now our pet person thinks we are, shall we say, plumpish. He is making us run on his treadmill and shows no signs of backing off. *Boring! Boring! Boring!* How can we escape this pet purgatory?

What, We're Plump?

Dear Plumpish:

First, it may help you to know that there is no difference between pooch pounds and human pounds. We can't eliminate your pain, but we may be able to reduce your distress.

We're sending you a complimentary copy of our self-help booklet, *Moderation for Mutts*. We also have a new app, *Treadmill Treasures*, you might like. It gives a video representation of your choice of twenty-five different critters, running at speeds keyed to your treadmill. We guarantee this will get your heart pumping! You can download a free copy from our website.

It will take time for your efforts to show results. When you've reached your goal, send us a selfie of the new yous.

Dear P. S. Pooch:

You've talked about healer hounds and guide dogs, but three of my siblings are therapy dogs. How confusing. Can you please elaborate?

Confused Chow

Dear Confused:

Sorry for the confusion. All three groups provide tremendous assistance to those they serve. Therapy dogs bring love, comfort, and distraction to those who are ill, depressed, lonely, or sad.

The main difference between the three groups lies in their qualifications and training. Healers rely on a natural gift possessed by only a select few. Guide dogs typically have months and years of training. Therapy dogs utilize their great personalities and warm hearts. It takes all three to make the world go round.

Karl K. Stevens, Ph.D.

Dear P. S. Pooch:

My older brothers go out every night and have fun with their friends. Mom says I can't go until I'm a year old, which won't be for another whole month! I tried to tell her that confinement is bad for my mental health, but she won't listen. She likes you guys and reads your column every day. Could you put in a good word for me?

Grounded

Dear Grounded:

The number one rule of puppyhood is that Mom knows best. She is just concerned about your health and safety.

A month will pass quickly. In the meantime, you may enjoy reading the enclosed copy of our booklet, *Puppy Proverbs*. We like number 7: "Patience is a virtue."

Dear P. S. Pooch:

The food my pet person gives me isn't exactly gourmet, if you catch my drift. She does give me a few treats, and they are quite tasty. If I ask for more, she calls me Moochie Poochie and lectures me about how treats are bad for my health. Help!

Deprived in Des Moines

Dear Deprived:

What a predicament! Many of the treats today actually are quite healthy. Look at the list of ingredients on the package or box. If you like what you see, show the list to your pet person. If that doesn't help or if your situation gets worse, you will have to resort to more drastic measures—like putting on your best sad face and going on an eating strike. This would be traumatic. Perhaps your friends can share some tasty tidbits while you and your pet person are working things out. Good luck!

Karl K. Stevens, Ph.D.

Dear P. S. Pooch:

I've been an avid reader of your columns since day one. Seems to me, and to some of my friends, that your later columns just aren't as biting as your earlier ones. Do you agree?

Keen Observer

Dear Keen:

Could it be that we are mellowing with age? Nah!